BOOTSY COLLINS
LEGENDARY LICKS

By Karl Kaminski

Recording credits:
Bass: Ivan "Funkboy" Bodley, www.funkboy.net
Keyboards: James Dower, www.jamesdower.com
Drums: Joe Goretti, www.joegoretti.com

Cover photo by Robert Knight

To access audio visit:
www.halleonard.com/mylibrary

Enter Code
7180-7846-8984-8345

ISBN 978-1-60378-150-3

Visit Hal Leonard Online at
www.halleonard.com

Contact us:
Hal Leonard
7777 West Bluemound Road
Milwaukee, WI 53213
Email: info@halleonard.com

In Europe, contact:
Hal Leonard Europe Limited
42 Wigmore Street
Marylebone, London, W1U 2RN
Email: info@halleonardeurope.com

In Australia, contact:
Hal Leonard Australia Pty. Ltd.
4 Lentara Court
Cheltenham, Victoria, 3192 Australia
Email: info@halleonard.com.au

Contents

Introduction

"Little did I know that I was doing it in stereo before stereo was a scenario."
– Bootsy Collins

William "Bootsy" Collins has created not only a persona, but also an instrument, a sound, a band, a style, and a culture. For the past 40 years, Bootsy has built a solid foundation for funk legends James Brown, George Clinton's Parliament/Funkadelic, his own group Rubber Band, as well as a full spectrum of recording artists, including Herbie Hancock, Keith Richards, Cyndi Lauper, Ice Cube, Dee-Lite, Snoop Dogg, the Red Hot Chili Peppers, Phil Ramone, Eddie Krammer, and Buddy Miles. In 1997, Bootsy was inducted into the Rock and Roll Hall of Fame, and in 2002 Bootsy finally got his first Grammy for his work with Fatboy Slim on "Weapon of Choice."

From the beginning, Bootsy Collins has been feeding his "creative monster" to get his own sound and music out to the world. Like Les Paul and Jimi Hendrix, he changed not only how we listen to music but how we play it as well. In 1970, when James Brown asked Bootsy what he wanted for his stage rig, Bootsy requested the unheard of: two Ampeg SVT amp heads with two 8x10 cabinets for each side of the stage. He reasoned that he just wanted everybody to "hear what he has to say, I mean play." Bootsy's goal has always been to dig deep to find that sound and bring something new to the party for the world to enjoy.

In *Bootsy Collins Legendary Licks*, we'll examine a dozen songs with Bootsy's bass lines and break the best licks down into learnable sections. In the Groove Primer section, there are sample scales that are found in Bootsy's bass lines, as well as a few rhythmic examples. The goal of this book is to bring you to a better understanding of Bootsy's style, as this will allow you to use his lines to develop your own ideas and grooves.

TRACK 1

Note: Track 1 contains tuning pitches.

About the Author

Karl Kaminski has been playing professionally throughout the United States, Japan, and the Caribbean for the past 30 years. He can be heard regularly around the NYC metro area with various jazz and pop groups. In addition to performing, Karl holds a master's degree in composition/arranging, teaches privately, and has authored various other projects. Some of his projects have included the play-a-long CDs for *Learn to Play Bass with Metallica: Volume 2*, and *Learn to Play Drums with Metallica: Volume 2*.

Photo by Jay Frederick

Acknowledgments

I would like to express my gratitude to Susan Poliniak for all of her guidance, and to Toby, Jay, Andy, Mike, and Wee for all of their musicianship, friendship, patience, and ears!

Gear Setup

Early Basses

Early on, Bootsy used a Fender Jazz with James Brown, as well as a Fender Precision with House Guests and the Funkadelic. In Rubber Band concert footage from 1976, two Fender basses can be seen at the front of the stage. By the mid '70s, Bootsy had already begun using the first Space Bass with Parliament.

Space Bass(es)

It seems that there are almost as many Space Basses as there are stars in the sky! Aside from the obvious star shape and the different finishes, each Space Bass is a 24-fret, four-string bass. One of the most unique aspects of the Space Bass is the electronics—the Space Basses have multiple sets of pickups with their own independent outputs. This allows for a wide range of tone control from each pickup. In general, the earlier Space Basses used Fender Precision pickups for the low and mid frequencies, and Fender Jazz pickups for the high frequencies. Later in the evolution of the bass, Bootsy included Bartolini Hi-A and EMG active pickups.

His Space Bass pickup configurations have included (from bridge to neck):

- Mid 1970s: Precision/Jazz/Jazz
- Late 1970s: Three Jazz sets (on two different Space Basses)
- Through 1980s: Three Humbucker sets (on two different Space Basses)
- Early 1990s: Three Precision sets
- Early 1990s: Active Jazz/Jazz/Active Humbucker/Jazz/Active Jazz
- Mid 1990s: Jazz/Jazz/Precision/Precision
- Through 2000s: Five Jazz sets

Currently, Warwick Basses out of Germany is designing a new Space Bass-3007. Bootsy's been told it will be able to admit astonishing sting-rays of sound and light that heal people immediately of all groovelessness and greedy tendencies of not being "on the One" with the Universe. We'll have to keep an eye and ear out for this cosmic tool of groove justice!

The Mother of All Rigs

"I was once asked by a prominent PA sound company, 'Why do I need a sound company when you carry your own PA system as a bass rig?' That was funny to me, but not to them—they felt intimidated as well they should!"—Bootsy Collins

The tendency of books such as this one is to list the gear of our heroes so that we can try to get our rig to sound just like theirs—or, at least, that's what we do for an *average* hero. Here, Bootsy is a stellar exception. He takes the bass-effect-amp configuration to the extreme! While his Space Bass is an integral part—and it gets a lot of attention—it's Bootsy's ingenious amp rig that creates his undeniable sound.

Bootsy's Space Bass uses multiple outputs to different amps for each of the high, mid, and low frequencies independently! In addition, each signal path is modified with its own set of effects, preamps, and power amps. The result is an incredibly customizable sound that is clean and powerful. Below is a sample of Bootsy's amp setup during his Parliament/Funkadelic/Rubber Band era. Notice how he splits and harmonizes the high frequencies while thickening the lows with octave and echo effects.

High-Frequency Signal Path

- Big Muff Fuzz
- Mu-Tron III
- MXR Digital Delay
- Morley Fuzz/Wah
- Morley Power Wah
- Eventide Harmonizer

The Eventide Harmonizer was in a box affectionately called R2FunkU. There was a keyboard in the box used to preset the harmonized intervals. It's easily recognizable in video footage by its "Can I Play?" sign.

The high frequencies were powered by an Alembic preamp, two Crown DC-300A amps, and four Cerwin-Vega V-32 speaker cabinets.

Mid-Frequency Signal Path

- Big Muff Fuzz
- Mu-Tron III
- MXR Digital Delay

Similarly, for the mids he used an Alembic preamp, two Crown DC-300A amps, and four Cerwin-Vega V-34s.

Low-Frequency Signal Path

- Mu-Tron Octave Divider
- Roland Space Echo
- Big Muff Fuzz
- Mu-Tron III

For the lows, he used three Acoustic 370 heads and six Cerwin-Vega cabinets. All of the CV cabinets coupled a large 18" speaker with a smaller speaker: Two cabinets combined an 18" with a 12" speaker, two more had an 18" with a 10", and the last two cabinets combined an 18" with an 8".

Since his 1991 tour with Dee-Lite, Bootsy's amp rig has grown to two 4x18, two 4x15, and four 8x10 cabinets powered by two Micro-Tech Crown 5000-watt amps, two QSC 4000-watt amps, two Micro-Tech Crown 3600-watt amps, and two Micro-Tech Crown 2500-watt amps, along with his four original Alembic preamps. While in the studio, he has been using a variety of Ampeg, SWR, Jonas Hellborg, and Hughes & Kettner amps, along with his custom cabinets.

News Flash!
Right now as this goes to press, Warwick is coming up with a plan to shake up the world of sound by inventing Bootsy a bass rig that will take us all the way up to the year 3007. Bootsy leaked the news saying, "By the time people catch up to how we did it, we'll be on other planets sharing our secrets!" Stay tuned to the Warwick website for details.

Effects

"Oh, I'll be a snowball in summertime, baby... Melt all over you!"

Bootsy is known for that sound—that sound that'll melt all over you. He gets it by splitting out the signal to parallel effects on different amps simultaneously. This alone would be a difficult undertaking for the average bassist, being that most of us play a mono-signal bass/amp rig. Bootsy still uses the same effects and original pedalboard as his recordings. Though the gear has aged, he swears by it and says that nothing sounds the same. Bootsy has noted, "Either I made the Mu-Tron famous or it made me famous. Either way, it was and still is the brand of my sound."

The following is Bootsy's basic effects chain setup. Keep in mind that this effects chain is repeated—with different settings—to four different amps! In addition to the effects chain, Bootsy always runs a direct signal *dry*, or without effects, to the house PA to add clarity and definition to the sound.

- Space Bass
- Mu-Tron
- Morley Fuzz-Wha
- Big Muff
- Mu-Tron Octavio
- MXR Digital Delay
- Roland Echoplex (later, Space Echo)
- Amplifier

While Bootsy's setup and vintage gear may be out of reach or hard to come by, here are the various basic effects that'll put you in the right solar system.

- Envelope filter, or auto-wah pedal
- Fuzz-wah
- Fuzz or overdrive pedal
- Octave pedal
- Delay pedal
- Harmonizer pedal
- Compression pedal

How you use each of these will depend on your bass and amp setup; you'll need to experiment with the chain order and placement. For the adventurous, you might even try an "A–B" pedal to broaden the possible tone paths. Another option is to run some effects between your bass and amp while placing other effects in the amp's built-in effects loop. Remember to balance your dry signal with the effects for clarity on the low end.

Sunglasses

Stars. "Twinkle, twinkle, baby!"

Groove Primer

The Meat

While rhythm may be the backbone of funk, you'll need to put some "meat" on that bone to make the music happen. Bootsy makes great use of minor pentatonic, blues, and dominant scales throughout his bass lines. For those of you who are new to these scales, you should focus on the second octave of each—the patterns of notes that fall on the A, D, and G strings. The tonic notes are shown as whole notes below, and you can move each of these scales around the neck. You'll need to get comfortable with each of them—they're in every song in one form or another!

Two-Octave E Minor Pentatonic Scale

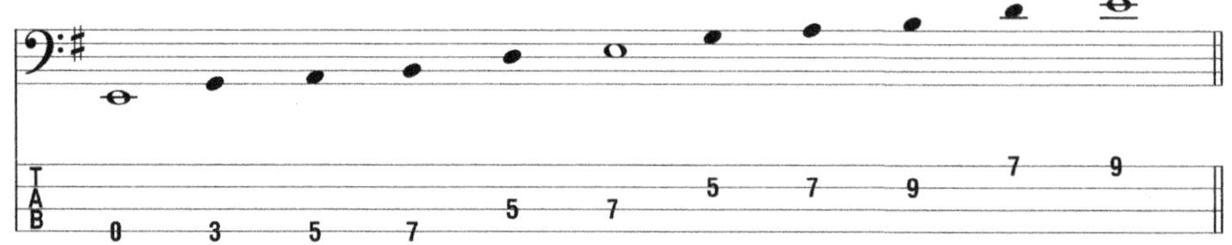

Two-Octave E Blues Scale

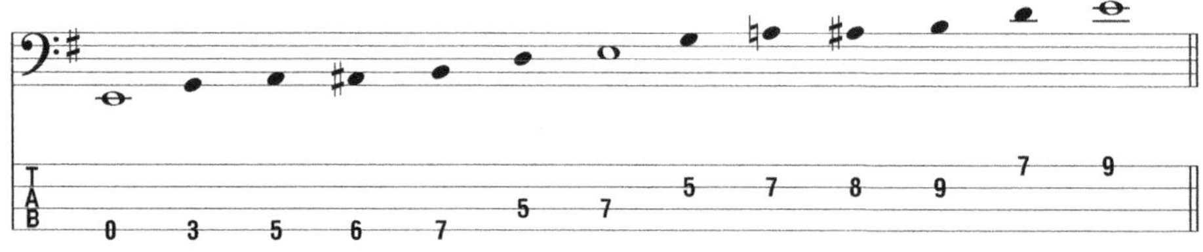

Two-Octave E Dominant Scale

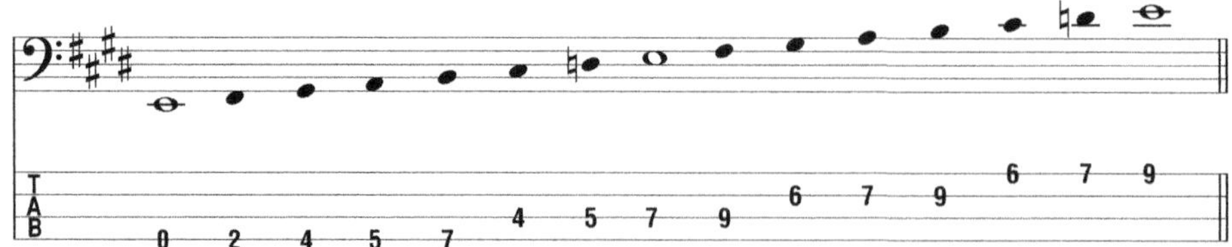

The Bone

Rhythm is the main ingredient in funk. You need to have a good sense of *syncopation*—playing off the beat—to achieve the right feel. Notice how the first beat of each example never changes: That's the core of the groove. Bootsy calls this playing "on the 1." The first beat must be strong on the beat. This is followed by varying fills. All of his bass lines use this kind of embellishment of the groove. Use a metronome and practice each of these examples to help you get a feel for the music. After you've played through all four examples separately, try playing them together, one after the other! By the way, these use combinations of the scales we looked at earlier.

TRACK 2

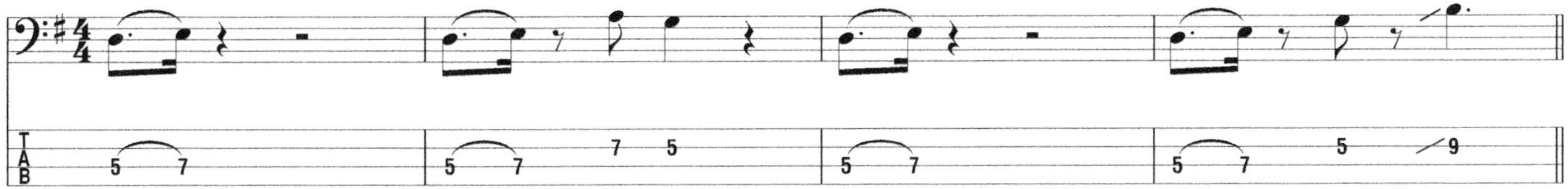

TRACK 3

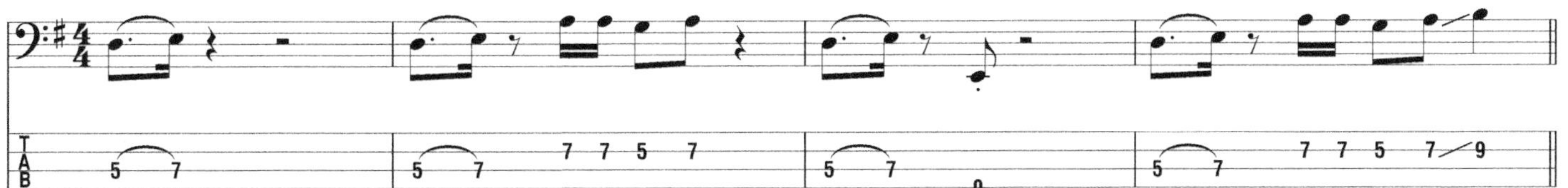

TRACK 4

TRACK 5

Stretchin' Out in a Rubber Band

from *Stretchin' Out in Bootsy's Rubber Band* (1976)

Words and Music by
William Earl Collins and George Clinton

The first track from Bootsy's debut Rubber Band album really sets the stage for his music for years to come. Bootsy's is definitely a bass-centric party. The groove is fat, funky, and right up-front throughout.

Intro and Verse Groove

The intro and verse are based on a four-bar phrase over an E minor pentatonic scale in the key of D major. Make sure to focus on the first three beats of measures 1 and 3, as that's the core of the groove. In the example, notice that the second bar of each four-bar phrase contains solo fills. Bootsy also adds a slight variation at the end of each phrase. Start in 5th position, keeping your fret hand in position so your left-hand index finger lines up with the 5th fret. (In this book, the left-hand fingers are referred to as index, middle, ring, and pinky.) Start all of the two-note pairs (D–E, F♯–G, etc.) with your index finger. Be careful not to attack the second note of each of the hammer-ons.

TRACK 6

Chorus

The chorus starts in the same position as the verse. Play the first note pair at the 5th fret, and then shift to the 3rd fret using your index finger on the low G and your ring or pinky finger on the high G. In measure 3, play the slide with both your ring and pinky fingers together; from now on I'll refer to this as the "ring-pinky combo." Play your slides short—about two frets from D to E and back again—as this will keep you in position for the G in beat 2 with your index finger. Start measure 4 with your index finger.

TRACK 7

Bridge

The bridge is more driving than the earlier groove sections. Try to keep the dynamics of the notes even so the accented notes at the end of each measure really pop the groove. Start in 5th position with your ring finger to play the descending chromatic line (E–E♭–D). At the end of measure 2, shift back up to the E with your index finger. Stay in position and stretch to the 10th fret using your pinky in measure 4. *Pop* the last note—play it with an upward plucking motion from under the string with your right-hand index finger.

In measure 9, the bass takes a lead/solo approach. (Note: For all examples, when counting measure numbers, count repeated measures twice.) Play the slides with the ring-pinky combo. In measures 12 and 14, start the triplets with your ring finger, shift your index finger to the G♯, and then finally shift to your middle finger for the G♮. Put a period at the end of the solo by popping that last note!

TRACK 8

Another Point of View

from *Stretchin' Out in Bootsy's Rubber Band* (1976)

Words and Music by William Earl Collins, George Clinton and Maceo Parker

The bass line to "Another Point of View" is very similar to "Stretchin' Out in a Rubber Band." The first beat is the core of the groove with various fills following it.

Intro Groove

The intro, which is based on an E minor pentatonic scale, is big and majestic like a classic power rock anthem. Start in 12th position with your ring finger on the A. Play the slide in measure 2 with your index finger, and then the slides in measure 3 with the ring-pinky combo. In measure 3, shift to the G in beat 3 with your middle finger; this puts you in position for the rest of measure 4. In measure 5, slide into the A with the ring-pinky combo and play the following G with your middle finger. Play the last slide with your index finger. Bootsy's tone is a little overdriven with a fuzz pedal on this one.

TRACK 9

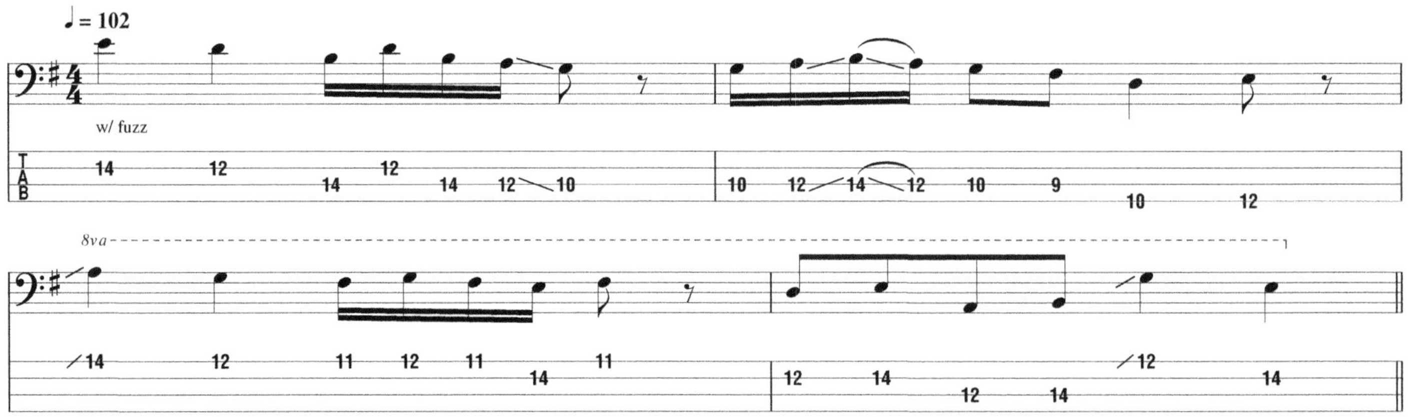

Verse Groove

Be sure to hit the verse strong on the downbeat, as the first beat of every measure is key to this groove. Just like in the last song, start in 5th position with your index finger. From here you'll be able to play all of the E blues scale fills. The only time you'll need to shift positions is in measure 4. Play the low G with your middle finger. The pickup to measure 6 is a great example of Bootsy's mastery of the feel—he adds variety while keeping the beat strong.

TRACK 10

Bridge Excerpt

The bridge section really starts to build with the layering of guitar, keys, and horns. There are some small but very relevant variations to the bass line to note here. Looking at the excerpt from the bridge, the bass line is really a repeated two-bar phrase with increasing complexity. In the first measure, check out the syncopation in beat 2 of the first phrase—that's the only time you'll see that in this section. He uses that like he's grabbing onto your collar and saying, "Hey, wait a minute baby! I got somethin' to show you!" It gets more complex in measures 9–12. Here, the line keeps the first two beats of the original phrase and ends with a roller coaster–like E blues scale lick. This one is definitely a keeper for your lick arsenal!

Start and stay in 5th position for the first eight measures. In measures 9–12, play the slides with the ring-pinky combo and stay there for the notes on the G string. In measure 10, play the A on beat 3 with your ring finger; this will put you in position for the next measure. In measure 12, shift up to the 14th fret with your ring (or pinky) finger, and shift back to play the last G in those measures with your index finger. Make sure that you *shift* from the A (12th fret) to the G (10th fret)—don't just slide down from the A!

TRACK 11

♩ = 102

End of the Chorus

At the beginning of the chorus, the bass *tacets*—drops out and does not play—for 18 bars. When Bootsy comes in, it's like a kick in the pants. He fills the void! The chorus is built on an E blues scale with an alternating slide to an E on either the A or G strings. This one will definitely build up your pinky strength!

The end of the chorus is a great example of how to use the full range of your bass to create a wider sound palette. Bootsy takes the opening phrase up the octave to the high B♭ on the G string. Start in 12th position and play the B♭ with your pinky. Be sure to pull off the second note, as this sets up a nice accented pattern. In beat 3, play all four notes in one pull-off; be sure to play the notes evenly. Play the slides with the ring-pinky combo, and play the following D in beat 1 with your index finger. Play the low notes on the E string in 3rd position.

TRACK 12

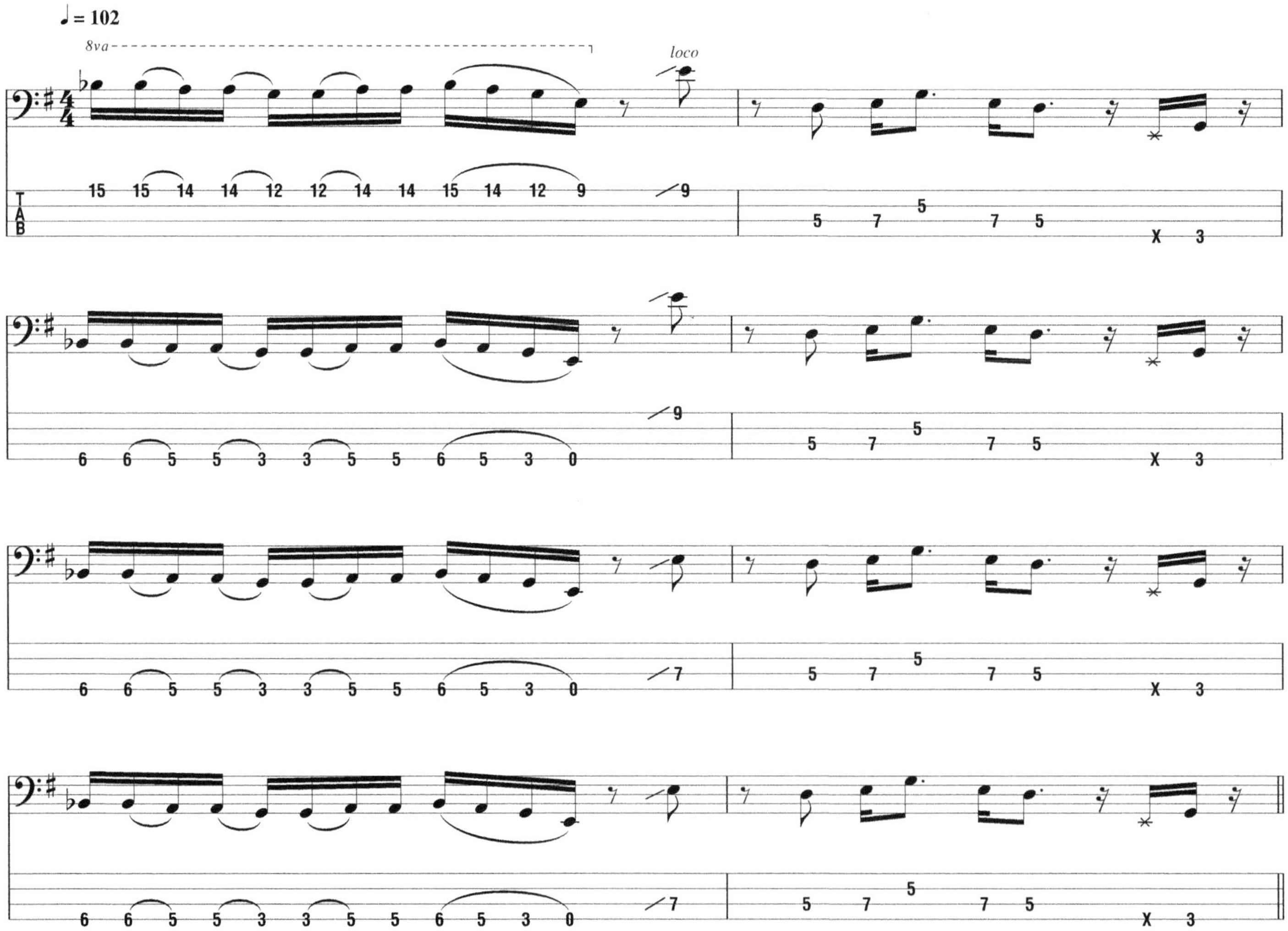

♩ = 102

8va – – – loco

15 15 14 14 12 12 14 14 15 14 12 9 /9 | 5 7 5 7 5 X 3

6 6 5 5 3 3 5 5 6 5 3 0 /9 | 5 7 5 7 5 X 3

6 6 5 5 3 3 5 5 6 5 3 0 /7 | 5 7 5 7 5 X 3

6 6 5 5 3 3 5 5 6 5 3 0 /7 | 5 7 5 7 5 X 3

Hollywood Squares

from *Bootsy? Player of the Year* (1978)

Words and Music by William Earl Collins,
Frank Waddy and George Clinton

Bootsy? Player of the Year is a pretty accurate statement. By the Rubber Band's third album, Bootsy was topping the charts alongside George Clinton's band Parliament—of which Bootsy was a high-profile member. It's no wonder that these guys were filling the charts. Bootsy's songs were getting more orchestrated and theatrical while still creating the atmosphere of a huge party where everyone was invited.

"Hollywood Squares" has one hell of a groove! After a dramatic fanfare-esque intro, the verse opens up with four bars of synth before the bass struts in. Bootsy's tone on this one is slightly overdriven with a mid-range bite—it's like he's out to getcha. Try to approach this bass line with a sense of freedom. If you get fixated on the shifts and the pops, it's gonna sound stiff!

Verse Groove

The verse groove is a two-bar phrase. Try to think of it as being broken up into two parts, like a kind of "call and response" groove. Be sure to nail beat 4 in the second measure—it's the only declarative downbeat! Use your thumb to "thump" or "slap" the notes on the A string of this section; the rest of the notes should be popped with your index finger. If you're new to slap technique, the general idea is to use the last knuckle of your thumb like a hammer to strike the string at the end of the fingerboard. Until you get the feel of it, you can attack the strings with your index and middle fingers.

Start with your ring-pinky combo on the C♯ and pull off to your index finger on the B. In beat 3, shift up to the D♯ with your index finger and play the E with your middle finger. In measure 2, repeat the same fingering for beat 1, and then shift to the E in beat 2 with your middle finger. This puts you in position to pop the next two notes. Use your index finger for the A♯ on the D string and your middle finger for the C♯ on the G string. Play the next C♯ in beat 3 with your index finger; this will set you up for the ring-pinky slide at the end of the lick. After the slide, it's a quick shift to C♯ on the A string with your ring-pinky combo.

In the last measure in the excerpt, there is a variation in the lick. Pop both of the notes on beat 4 and end with a hammer-on. The rest is funk and repeat!

TRACK 13

Bridge

The bridge is the same orchestral fanfare as the intro, only now it's now updated with an intimate "Hollywood lounge" vibe. To get into that sexy groove, you'll need to use your index finger to "drag" each note down after the attack. Despite the fact that you're "dragging" the notes down, don't drag the rhythm down with it! This section is played on the beat, so it's important to lock into beats 1 and 3—just listen to the bass drum. Ultimately, you end this section by popping the C♯ on the G string. Be sure to play it *staccato*, or really short. There's a key change here, so all of the A notes are now natural.

TRACK 14

Chorus Groove

The bass drops out for the first four bars of the chorus. Bootsy's line here is really tight and rhythmical. You'll need to *pizz*—play with your "pickhand" fingers to attack the strings—closer to the bridge to get that tight sound and feel. Don't freak out over the rhythm in beat 1. Play these like regular 16th notes, but try to make them "skip" or "swing." Play beat 2 short and don't forget all of the accented notes in beat 4 of each measure. The downbeats of beat 1 and 2 as well as the accented note in beat 4 are the core of the groove here.

In measure 9, Bootsy adds another twist: Beat 1 is now a 16th note sextuplet. Unlike the tuplet in the earlier feel, you'll need to play this as even as possible. The key lies in the articulation. Attack the muted note with your index finger and the first note of the sextuplet with your middle finger, and then *rake* with your index finger—drag it to attack the adjacent string—to hit the next two notes. Repeat for the second half of the sextuplet: middle, index–rake–index.

Be aware of the key change, as now all of the A and E notes are sharp. The whole section is over C♯ major pentatonic. You'll be able to play it using an A♯ minor pentatonic fingering based on the 6th fret of the E string.

TRACK 15

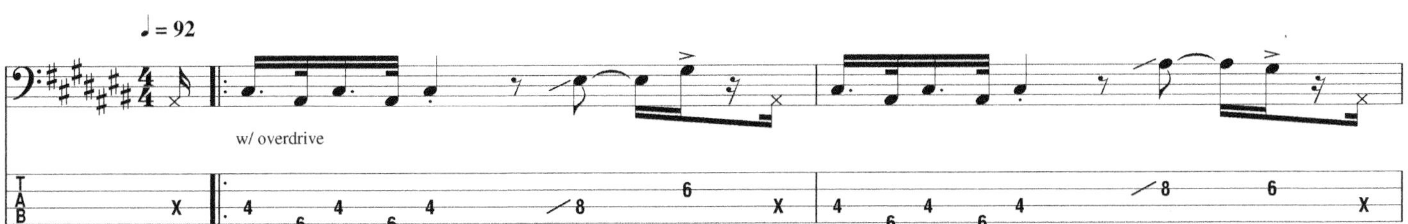

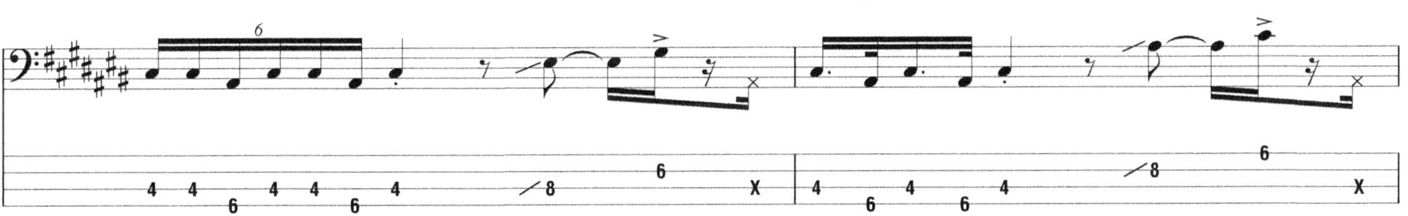

F Encounter

from *Ultra Wave* (1980)

Words and Music by William Earl Collins, Ronald Ford, Richard Lee Evans and George Clinton

Ultra Wave was Bootsy's fifth release. Even though the personnel still consisted of P-Funk players, this release was just listed as "Bootsy Collins" and not the Rubber Band. This recording certainly has a different tone to it, both on the bass and otherwise. *Ultra Wave* is thick with keyboards, and the bass is not as transparent. While the grooves are still incredibly solid, at times the bass gets lost in a fog of electronica.

Bootsy's tone on this track is thick and watery with a little bit of bite to it—almost synth-like. He uses a lot of slides to add to the effect. You'll definitely need to favor the mid-range of your bass and use an envelope filter or octave pedal for this one.

Intro

Start the intro in 2nd position and play all of the B slides with your ring-pinky combo on the E string. In measure 2, shift up the the A on the 5th fret with your index finger; this will set you up for the B slide in measure 3.

TRACK 16

♩ = 109

Verse/Chorus Excerpt

The verse/chorus section is a great example of how to expand your ideas. Bootsy takes the core elements of the intro groove—the strong downbeats "on the 1" in the first and third bars—and fills in the space with expanded F♯ blues scale licks and more slides. In this section, continue to play the E-string slides with your index finger, but play the slides on the A string with a ring-pinky combo. Pay attention to all of the open-string hammer-ons and pull-offs—even though they happen quickly, they really add to the groove.

TRACK 17

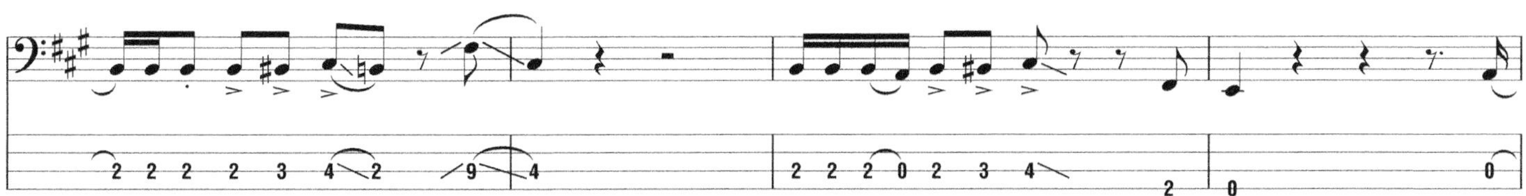

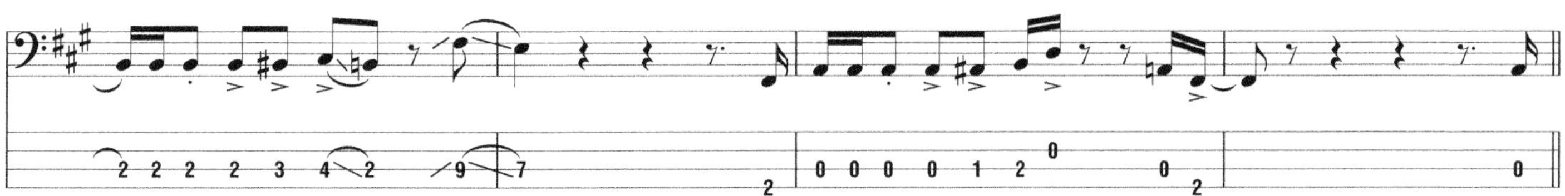

Bridge

The bridge continues in 2nd position for the first eight bars. Most of the slides in the bridge are played with your ring-pinky combo. Keeping your fingers together will help support your slide, as this will come in handy for the big E-string slide in measure 12. In measure 8, shift to the B with your middle finger. The notes in measure 9 follow a B dominant scale pattern.

The E on beat 1 of measures 10 and 14 should be played with your middle finger. At the ends of measures 11 and 15, play the E-note slides with your index finger.

TRACK 18

It's a Musical

from *Ultra Wave* (1980)

Words and Music by William Earl Collins,
Carl Small and George Clinton

The tone on this one is a nice, gain-y, Precision-type sound. Use your neck pickup with the gain up high. Here again, Bootsy's inventive use of effects creates a psychedelic carnival of tones. His sound is multi-layered with triggered effects and delay. The dry sound with wah is panned left, and the wet sound (envelope filter, Space Echo, etc.) is panned right. Throw in Bootsy's added sliding bass lines and the overall effect is dizzying!

Intro

The four-bar intro is based on a G minor pentatonic scale. Attack the strings close to the bridge to get a tight percussive sound, and play the opening hammer-on with your index finger. At the end of the measure, shift your index finger to the 5th fret to play the grace note hammer-on. In beat 3 of the third measure, shift up to the 10th fret to catch the end of the phrase. Play the last slide short to about the 7th fret so that you'll be in position for the next phrase.

TRACK 19

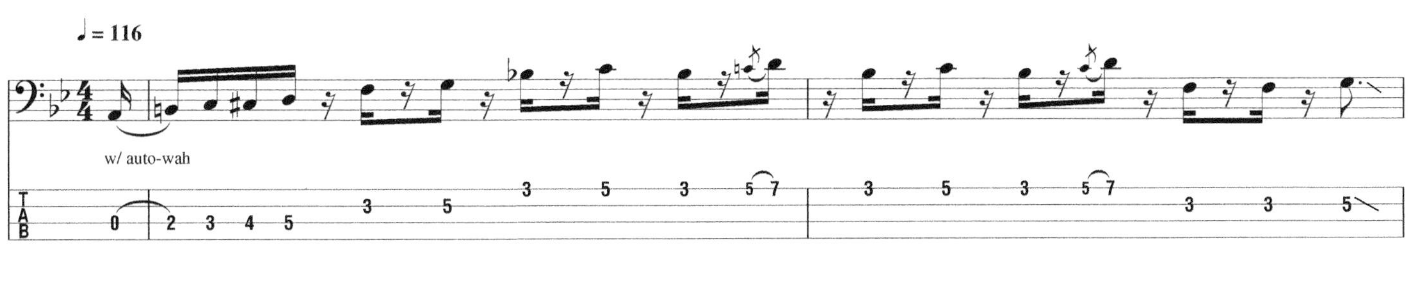

Verse Excerpt

The best way to digest this is to break it up into small, two-bar chunks. It's really just a repeated two-bar groove over an E minor pentatonic scale. The core of the groove is the eighth notes in the first two beats of bar 1 (and all of the odd measures). In bar 2 (and all of the even measures), Bootsy fills with a variety of slaps, pops, and slides. While the fills may be exciting, make sure that you focus on the downbeat of bar 1. If you lose that, then there is no groove!

Basically, start all of the phrases with your pinky or ring finger. All of the octave intervals are played with your index finger on the root and your ring-pinky combo for the octave (two frets up, two strings over). This excerpt is played with the thumb, and all of the G-string notes are popped. The slides are played with either your index finger or ring-pinky combo.

Bootsy's use of the slide is as an expressive voice like a sigh, a shout, or a moan. In general, the majority of the slides should be played or started with your index finger. There are primarily three types of slides here: adjacent-string slides, single-string slides, and single-note slides. When a slide is played on a string and then switched to an adjacent string at the same fret, the slide should be played with the same finger, as in measures 4, 6, 7, etc. When two slides follow each other on the same string, the slides should be played with opposite fingers, meaning that if you start a slide up with your index finger, the following slide down should be played with your ring-pinky combo, as in measure 11. The remaining slides are standard single-note slides.

TRACK 20

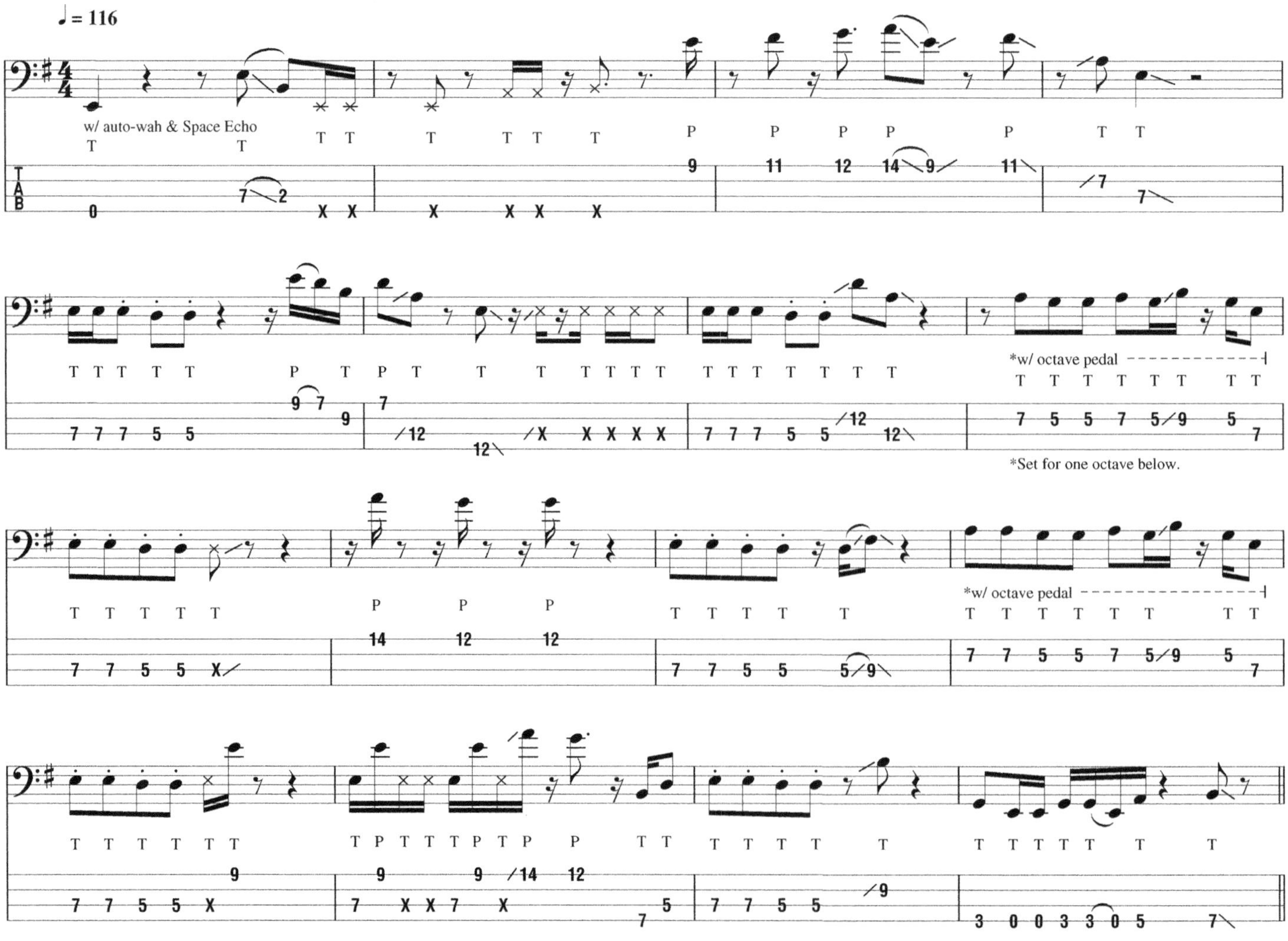

♩ = 116

w/ auto-wah & Space Echo

*w/ octave pedal

*Set for one octave below.

Chorus

The chorus, like the intro, is based on a G minor pentatonic lick. In measure 1 (and all of the odd measures), play the 5th-fret notes with your pinky and the 3rd-fret notes with your index finger. In measure 2 (and all of the even measures), play the octave phrases with your index finger on the E string and your ring finger or pinky on the D string. Be sure to attack only the first note of the open-string hammer-ons and the slides.

TRACK 21

Fat Cat

from *Ultra Wave* (1980)

Words and Music by
William Earl Collins and Phelps Collins

As mentioned earlier, the general sound of Bootsy's bass on *Ultra Wave* is a lot more electronic and layered than his earlier recordings. This bass part is doubled with a bass synth, and the rolling bass fills in the chorus are monstrous!

In general, this is a classic Bootsy groove—a tight, 16th-note groove played "on the 1." Be sure that all of the phrases lead to the strong downbeat of beat 1.

Intro

Bootsy's intro is a slithery solo of slides and vibrato. Notice how he uses a bass fill to lead into not only the following downbeat but the root of each chord as well. Play the slides in the first two measures with your ring-pinky combo. In measure 2, use your index finger to play both the E and the F. Be careful not to slide between the two notes! Play the rest of the intro on the D string. Use vibrato for the Cs in measure 2 and the F and G in measure 4. To get a good vibrato, push the string into the fingerboard and bend it towards the floor, letting the string "ride" on the fret. Keep applying pressure with your thumb as you bend. Vibratos can be fast or slow, as well as deep (wide) or shallow (narrow). In this case, they are fast and shallow.

TRACK 22

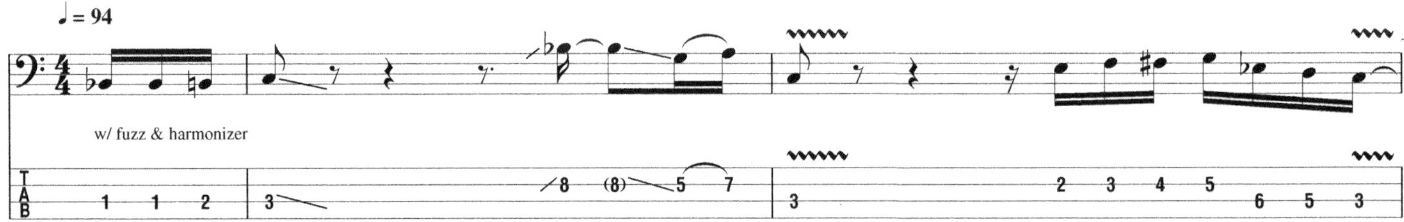

Verse Groove

The verse is a two-bar groove based on a Cm7–Fm7–Gm7 chord progression. The bass line is played in 1st position and built around the notes of each chord arpeggio as well as a C blues scale at the 3rd fret. The only time you'll need to shift is for the notes on the 5th fret in measures 4 and 6. In measure 4, play the last C with your index finger and shift back to 1st position for the B♭ in measure 5. Notice how Bootsy mixes ascending and descending licks—this is a great way to add variety to your grooves without losing the feel.

TRACK 23

End of Pre-Chorus

Like the verse, the pre-chorus is just a repeated two-bar groove in A minor. This excerpt is from the end of the pre-chorus leading into the next section. Start in 2nd position, and play the first bar of the groove with your index finger for the B in beat 2. In the second bar of the groove, shift to 1st position to play the rest of the bar using your middle finger for the B in beat 2. Repeat the groove by shifting back up to 2nd position.

To lead into the next section, start the C chromatic line in beat 3 of measure 4 with your index finger. Play the four chromatic notes in beat 3 with each finger in order—index, middle, ring, pinky. Similarly, in beat 4 shift to the E on the D string and play the next four notes starting again with your index finger followed by middle, ring, and pinky.

TRACK 24

Chorus Fills

Similar to the intro, this section is built around solo bass fills that lead into a strong downbeat. The core of the groove here is the riff in measures 2, 4, 6, and 8. Make sure you lock in on the 16th-note phrase (B–A–B–C) leading to beat 2. Start this section in 7th position. In measure 2, play the slides with your ring-pinky combo and attack only the B notes in the pull-offs and hammer-ons. Play the G in beat 3 with your index finger. The bass fill in measure 3 is an A minor pentatonic scale. Stay in 5th position until the E–D slide in beat 2. Play the slide with your ring-pinky combo. This will set up your index finger for the following C. In measure 4 (as well as measures 6 and 8), play the slides in beat 1 with your index finger in 2nd position. Lead into the next bass fill in measure 5 with a ring-finger slide so you'll be in position for the three-note groupings on each string. Play the last slide with your index finger. The final bass fill in measure 9 is again an A minor pentatonic lick, only this time it's played in open position. Play the opening B–C slide with your pinky, and then the rest of the lick is in 2nd position using the open strings.

TRACK 25

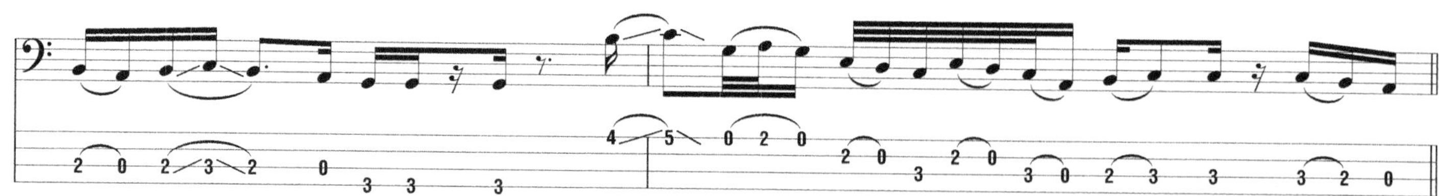

Bridge Excerpt

The bridge is based on a repeated four-bar phrase and makes use of both the D blues and D minor pentatonic scales for the fills. In general, you should play the first two bars in 1st position and play the third and fourth bars in 2nd position. In the first bar, play the slides into beat 2 with your ring finger. In the second bar, shift to 3rd position in beat 4 (except for measure 2, where you should stay in 1st position to play the C–B♭–C on the A string).

There are three fills to note in this section. In measure 7, shift to 5th position on beat 2 to play the D blues scale lick. In measure 12, slide up to the A with your pinky and down to the F with your index finger. Be sure to catch all of the pull-offs in this D minor pentatonic fill. And in measure 16, there's a rolling fill that starts as a D minor pentatonic lick and ends as a D blues scale lick. Start measure 16 with a slide up to the C on the D string with your pinky, and then play the following A–G slide with your index finger. After playing the D on the A string, shift to 3rd position to start the D blues scale in beat 3. Play the G–A♭–G slide with your ring-pinky combo and pull off to your index finger for the F. Again, you'll need to make sure that you catch the hammer-on/pull-off phrases—they make the lick flow!

TRACK 26

♩ = 94

w/ fuzz & harmonizer

Landshark
(Just When You Thought It Was Safe)

from *The One Giveth, the Count Taketh Away* (1982)

Words and Music by
William Earl Collins and Phelps Collins

"Just when you thought it was safe" is right—Bootsy's sound has grown! Two years after the *Ultra Wave* album, Bootsy released *The One Giveth, the Count Taketh Away.* The flamboyant and provocative album cover is a good preview of what you're about to get: a face full of bass! Not only is Bootsy's trademark juicy sound tighter and deeper than his previous albums, but he's also slapping and popping more. Up until now, Bootsy's sound had been buried behind the effects and layered into the mix; here you can hear the dry and wet signals within the mix. The bass is sparkling and bright.

Opening Groove

"Landshark" hits you in the face with full-force funk. As is standard for a big groove, it's "on the 1." There are a lot of slides and popping here, but nothing is more important than hitting those phrases on the downbeat of the measure, so don't be distracted by the line. The best way to get around this line is to have a good sense of the octave and stay in position, keeping each of your fingers lined up with the frets so that you can play the same finger on adjacent and cross-string phrases. Measure 1 is a great example. While you're playing a slide and across three strings, you need to keep your hand in 7th position so that you can reach all of the upper phrases. The groove is a two-bar phrase, and all of the licks are built on the E minor and E minor pentatonic scales. Work through two or four bars at a time.

Watch out for the slides, too. Bootsy uses slides as melodies as well as percussive shouts. Regardless of where they may rhythmically start or end, they are essentially markers for the downbeats. The peak of a slide typically lands on the beat. You'll see this in a lot of Bootsy's lines emphasizing beats 1 and 3 or 2 and 4, depending on the groove of the song. In addition, his slides aren't random notes—they tend to use the root, 5th, and octave of the chord. Beginning in measure 9, there is a series of slides; focus on the fact that they "pulse" the downbeats. Most of them are played with the index finger. The longer slides that come back down can be played up with the index and then dragged back down with the ring-pinky combo.

TRACK 27

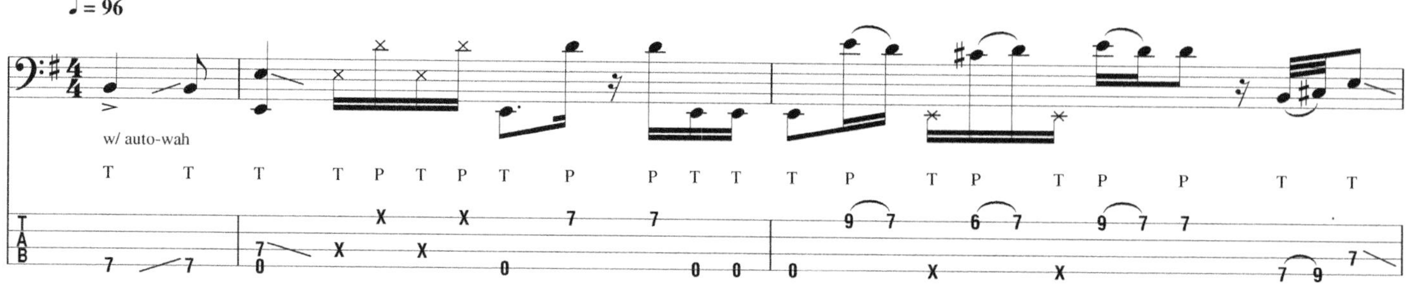

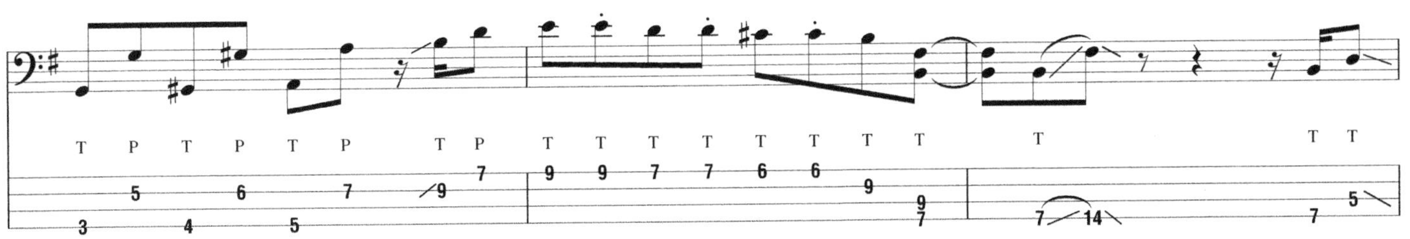

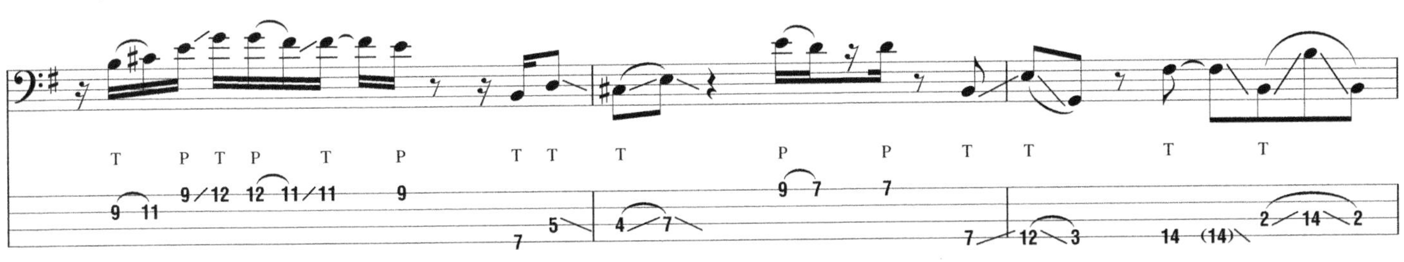

First Verse Excerpt

The first verse is much more laid back than the previous section. Keep in mind that the pull-offs and hammer-ons are the most important elements here. In measure 16, play the double stops strong with your index finger on the root (lower note) and your ring-pinky combo on the 5th (upper note) of each chord.

TRACK 28

♩ = 96

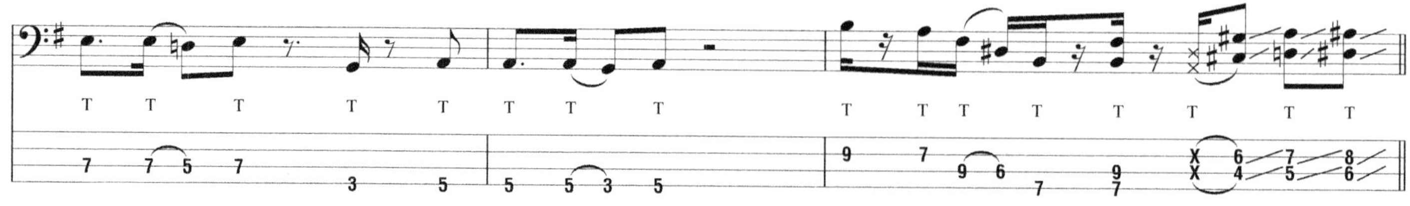

Second Chorus Excerpt

The second chorus is the same two-bar groove as before. Note that the two-bar phrase is played three times, and then a fourth time with climbing octaves. This creates an eight-bar phrase that repeats, so even though there is a lot of variation to the bass line, it does follow a distinct pattern. Keep this in mind when you're developing your own bass grooves: Start with a solid two-bar groove and develop it into four- and eight-bar phrases.

In measure 1, there is an open-palm slap on all of the strings. Bootsy jokingly calls it "hitting my baby on the butt." Just slap down with the palm of your hand onto the face of your bass to hit all of the strings at once. Mute the strings with your palm after each hit. Try not to lift your palm up—this should sound percussive, not ringing.

Soloing over the Verse Groove

The second verse is more complex and illustrates how Bootsy uses rhythmic ideas to lead to "the 1." Go back and compare this example to the excerpt of the first verse. You can clearly see that while playing a lot of fills, Bootsy never abandons the downbeat or the root of each chord. Listening to the album, you'll hear that even as Bootsy is playing complementary counter-line fills to the guitar solo, he's still laying down a solid groove.

Play the fills in measure 12 (B minor pentatonic) and measure 16 (B dominant scale) at the 7th fret.

TRACK 30

Ever Lost Your Lover

from *Fresh Outta "P" University* (1997)

Words and Music by
Johnny Davis and William Earl Collins

"Ever Lost Your Lover" is one of the more recent tracks from Bootsy's collection, and certainly the most contemporary tune in this book. While all of Bootsy's trademark funk elements are there (strong, bass-driven groove; thick, liquid bass tone; solid backbeat) this tune really crosses over into R&B with Bootsy's smooth vocals, slick horns, and moody harmony. Don't be fooled—there's no Pinocchio Theory here (Bootsy's theory about faking the funk). You'll dance with your baby all night.

Main Groove

The opening eight-bar riff is a deep, solid groove. This bass line is all about getting in position to play the cross-string octave pattern. You'll need to break out your auto-wah pedal and nail 1 and 3 in each measure. You can think of this groove as a four-bar phrase where just the last two notes are different. The main groove is used for the intro, verses, and choruses.

In measures 1 and 5, play the first three 16th notes with your index, middle, and ring fingers, respectively. Follow up with your pinky for the G on the D string. Shift back down to the F in beat 3 with your index finger. In the rest of the measures, use your index finger to slide up to the second note. You'll be in position for the following note an octave above it. Play the muted notes in measures 2 and 4 by simply laying your fingers flat on the string without pressing down. In measure 8, play beat 3 with your index finger. Finally, play the slides at the end of measures 4 and 8 on the E string. This will give you a longer, thicker-sounding slide.

TRACK 31

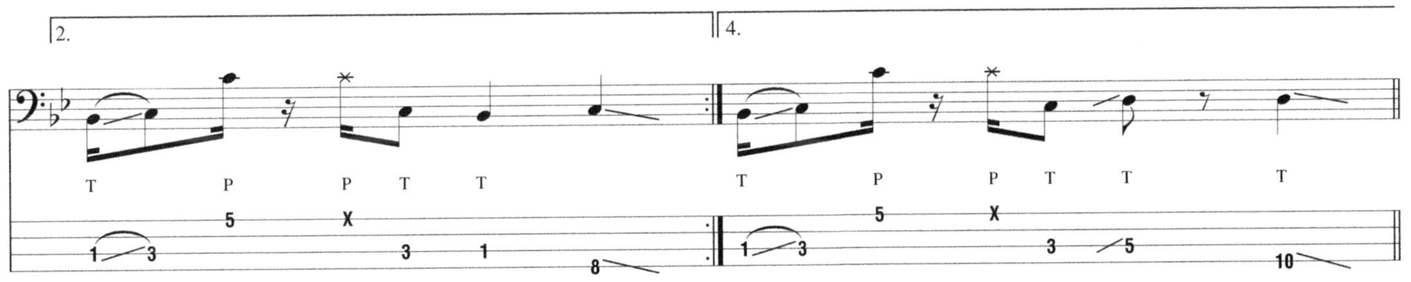

Bridge

The bridge is really just a variation of the opening bass line following a slightly different harmony and adding popping lines in measures 5–8. Approach the first four bars like the verse, only the harmony is G to D instead of G to C. In measure 5, play the slides on the A string with your index finger and the slide on the G string with your ring-pinky combo. In beat 3, be sure to reach back for that D–E♭ slide. In measure 8, slide into beat 1 with your pinky, and then play the downbeats of 2 and 3 with your index finger, and the slide in beat 4 with your ring-pinky combo on the E string.

TRACK 32

End of the Second Bridge

One of the toughest things to do as a bassist is to just lock in to the groove without distraction. A true master picks his moment to fill. I added one of those moments here in this excerpt from the second time through the bridge. The first six measures of the second bridge are the same as first bridge—only the last two are different. In the first of these two measures, Bootsy adds a group of muted notes to the groove. Play this measure as before, with a slide in beat 1 and add the muted notes. Be careful to play the last two muted notes evenly with your thumb. Play the A–B♭ slide in beat 3 with your index finger, as this sets you up for the following F. Play the G slide in beat 4 with your pinky.

TRACK 33

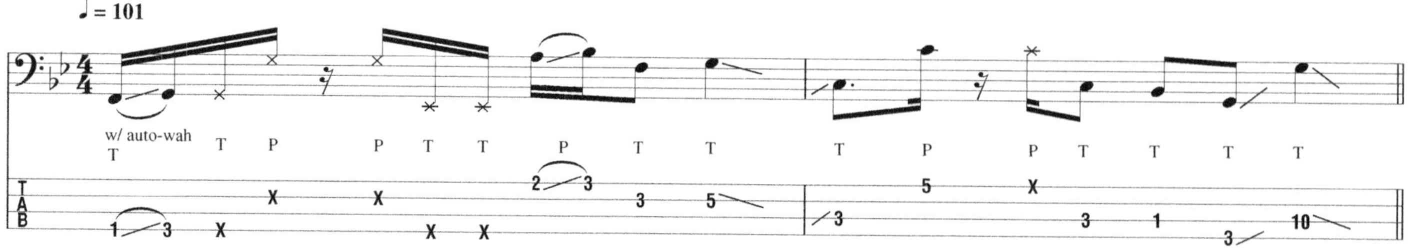

Vamp-Out Groove

Here again, the vamp is based on the main groove but moves over a new harmony: Am–D7–Gm–C7. Play the first slide in each measure with your index finger shifting positions as needed. Play the slides at the ends of the measures with your ring-pinky combo.

TRACK 34

Bootzilla

from *Bootsy? Player of the Year* (1978)

Words and Music by
William Earl Collins and George Clinton

"Bootzilla" is an introduction to yet another of Bootsy personas—the world's only rhinestone rock star doll. The tone is juicy and thunderous. If you're lucky enough to own a Mu-Tron pedal, power it up. If not, you'll need an auto-wah, envelope filter, or harmonizer to thicken your sound.

Main Groove

The song opens up with a dream-like, eight-bar children's song, which goes into jarring, rolling E notes leading to the main groove. The main groove enters in eight-bar phrases. This section is played over an F♯ minor pentatonic scale in 2nd position. Play the low F♯ slides with your index finger—squeeze every bit of slide out of that note!

TRACK 35

♩ = 104

w/ auto-wah & harmonizer

Chorus Excerpt

The chorus is a repeated four-bar groove over an F♯ dominant scale. For this section, you'll need to shift up to the 7th fret on the A string with your pinky and back down to the 2nd fret of the E string with your middle finger in almost every measure. In measures 4 and 8, shift up the D string to play the A♯ in the following measures. In measure 8, shift up to the 4th fret with your index finger to play the pickup to beat 4 (C♯–G♯–C♯) and shift up to the A♮ at the end of the measure with your middle finger.

TRACK 36

End of the Chorus

Throughout this book, we've looked at a lot of Bootsy's legendary licks. But in my opinion, the transition to the last eight bars of the chorus is what it's all about! Up to this point, the chorus has been a four-bar groove based on beats 1 and 3. In the next eight bars, the groove opens up into a four-bar solo-istic riff based on the quarter note, and emphasizing beats 2 and 3. If the technical description sounds confusing, just watch how your body moves as you listen to the transition on the album. That's the funk right there!

As in the previous section, this is over an F♯ dominant scale in 1st position. Play the hammer-on/pull-off combinations on the A string using your middle finger for B♯ and your ring-pinky combo for the C♯–A pull-off.

TRACK 37

Give Up the Funk
(Tear the Roof off the Sucker)

from *Mothership Connection* (Parliament, 1975)

Words and Music by George Clinton Jr.,
William "Bootsy" Collins and Jerome Brailey

This is the funk anthem. It's probably the biggest hit from the album, and certainly the most recognizable Parliament hit altogether. Musicians and non-musicians alike can easily sing along to this danceable party classic. Bootsy's sound on this song is that Precision-type tone—fat and warm. Use your neck pickup with your tone control set to dark.

Opening Lead Riff

This opening eight-bar section features the bass in a series of two-bar minor pentatonic licks. While it may look complicated, it's really all the same notes; you just change direction. Stay in 7th position and play all of the 7th-fret notes with your index finger and all of the 9th-fret notes with your pinky. You'll need to shift at the end of each two-bar phrase. In beat 4 of measures 2, 4, and 6, shift back to the 5th-fret D with your index finger. Play the D–E and rake the open E string. While playing this open E string, shift to the 9th fret with your index finger for the F♯–G hammer-on. Again, you'll follow up with a rake of the open E string and then, while playing this note, quickly shift to the next A on the D string with your index finger. This sets you up for the next two-bar phrase. Be sure to attack only the first note of each hammer-on, and play the notes short where indicated—the staccato style adds percussiveness to the bass line.

TRACK 38

Refrain Riff

The refrain, "We want the funk!" contains the classic bass line that everyone knows. It's based on an E dominant scale and can be heard through the majority of the song. Start with your pinky for the E at the 7th fret, and remember to use all of your fingers on the A string to help support the pinky. The key to this section is in the phrasing. Play beat 1 long and beat 3 short. The muted note is played in position on the 4th fret—simply touch the string firmly without pressing down. Finally, the last open E in measure 2 comes just after the downbeat of beat 4.

TRACK 39

Refrain Riff with Fills

Bootsy's basic "get in a groove and play the funk" is illustrated here. It's all about laying down a core groove and filling around it without getting in the way or loosing the feel. The refrain riff continues here, only Bootsy adds a tritone to mimic the "do" of the singers in beat 1 of measure 3 and again in beat 4 of measure 5. Complementing other sections of the band in your bass grooves is a great way to add depth to your playing. This is a fundamental yet important concept to remember when you make up your own funk lines.

Play the interval on the D and G strings with your index and middle fingers. Use your index finger on the D and your middle finger for the G♯. It may feel awkward, but it's easy once you get used to it. Make your slides short and quickly shift back to the 4th fret for the muted note.

TRACK 40

Ahh... The Name Is Bootsy Baby

from *Ahh... The Name Is Bootsy Baby* (1977)

Words and Music by William Earl Collins, George Clinton and Maceo Parker

For those who still didn't get it, the title track off the Rubber Band's second release was an introduction to the world. From the perspective of two new concertgoers, we experience Bootsy's Rubber Band first-hand from the opening of the concert to meeting Bootsy backstage where he offers some playful answers to inquiring minds. During the concert, Bootsy also introduces us to Casper, one of his earliest personas. By this time, Bootsy had expanded his sound beyond fuzz and delay. Some of the effects even start to play active character roles in the music. For instance, Casper is conjured up with the use of a Roland Space Echo to say a friendly "boo."

Opening Lick and Main Groove

The opening two bars is a unique 5/4 phrase. Start this one with your index finger and be sure to count! The main groove is a two-bar riff in 4/4. By the second repeat of the groove, the downbeat of bar 1 becomes syncopated and the second bar remains on the 1.

TRACK 41

Bass 2 Fills

"Ahh... The Name Is Bootsy Baby" includes multiple/overdubbed bass tracks. The bass fills (labeled Bass 2) are two-bar phrases over a D minor pentatonic scale. Start at the 3rd fret and shift up to the fills on the 7th with your ring-pinky combo. In measure 7, use a delay/echo for Casper's "boo" at the 19th fret.

The main groove continues on the bottom staff (labeled Bass 1) during the fills. The only variation to the main groove is the addition of a rising F♯–G–A in measure 4.

TRACK 42

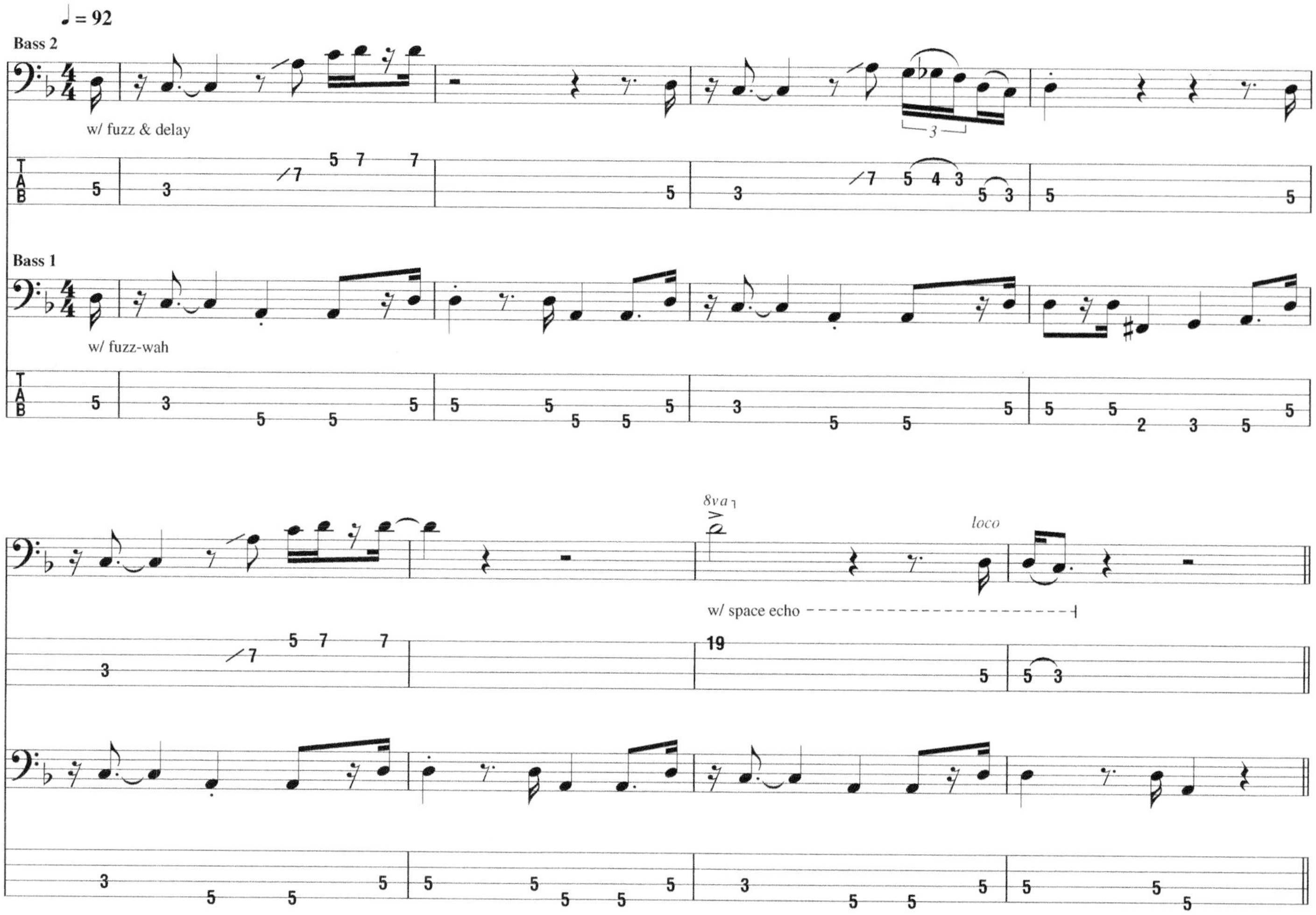

♩ = 92

Bass 2

w/ fuzz & delay

Bass 1

w/ fuzz-wah

8va

loco

w/ space echo

Bridge Riff

The bridge continues in 2nd position over a D dominant scale. On beat 3 of measure 2, shift up to the 7th fret with your index finger, as this will prepare you for the A-string slide with your ring-pinky combo. In measure 4, shift up to the A with your pinky and pull off to your index finger for the vibrato.

TRACK 43

Bass 2 Solo

This song is just a big party in two parts: the main groove and the bridge. After the bridge, the song returns to a similar Bass 2 fills section. This time, Bass 2 opens up into a solo. Again, most of this is played at the 3rd fret and then shifts up to the 7th fret with your ring-pinky combo. In measures 4–5, use your index finger for the popped notes on the G string. In measures 8–9, play the open-palm slap muted across all of the strings at the end of the fingerboard, and avoid letting the strings ring and vibrate. Use delay/echo for the popped notes of Casper's "boo" in measures 14–20.

Bass 1 continues to play the main groove underneath the solo, similar to the Bass 2 Fill section.

TRACK 44

Melodic Soloing

At the end of the song, Bootsy cuts into a distorted solo rendition of "Auld Lang Syne" similar in feel to Jimi Hendrix's version of "The Star Spangled Banner." In this example, Bootsy shows his talents as a soloist beyond the scope of bass grooves, riffs, and fills.

This example is over a B minor pentatonic scale; it switches to a D minor pentatonic scale at measure 24. Play all of the slides with your ring-pinky combo and simply follow the melody through the minor pentatonic fingerings. In measures 1–24, use your index finger to play the A-string Ds with the exception of measures 8, 16, and 24: Here, shift your index finger to the 3rd fret to play the D–C–D–C phrase. In measure 24, stay in 3rd position for the next melodic phrase—use your index finger for the D-string Fs. Play the G–F slide in measure 25 with your index finger.

Up for the Down Stroke

from *Up for the Down Stroke* (Parliament, 1974)

Words and Music by George Clinton Jr., William "Bootsy" Collins and Bernard G. Worrell

This title track from Parliament's second album was their first chart-topper, and it remains one of their most popular songs. In true Parliament fashion, this is a party call-to-war with a thunderous groove.

Opening and Chorus Groove

The bass tone on this one is another classic Precision sound. Use your neck pickup and a fuzz-wah effect. Play the opening four-bar intro on the E string with your thumb, and shift to the F♯ on the G string with your ring finger.

The chorus groove (starting at measure 5) is a repeating two-bar phrase using both E dominant and minor pentatonic scales. Focus on the pickup B and downbeat D–E at the beginning of each two-bar phrase (measures 5, 7, 9, and 11). The majority of this excerpt is played at the 5th fret with shifts up to 9th position on the G string every four bars. The slides are all played with your ring-pinky combo except for the slide in measure 10. Play this one by sliding up to the 7th fret with your index finger.

TRACK 46

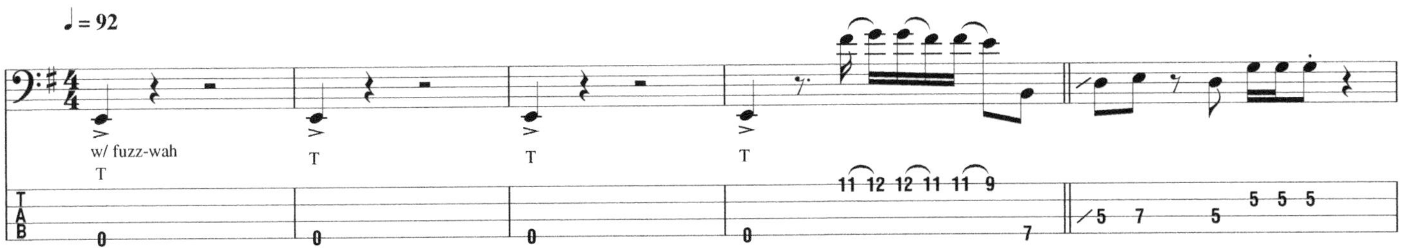

Bridge Riff

The bridge riff is just a repeated two-bar phrase over an A dominant scale played in 4th position. The only shift you'll need to make is in beat 4 of the second bar. Shift to the G♮ on the E string with your index finger. Shift back up to your middle finger for the A to repeat the phrase. This groove is more syncopated than the chorus, so be sure to play the low A just after the downbeat of each bar.

TRACK 47

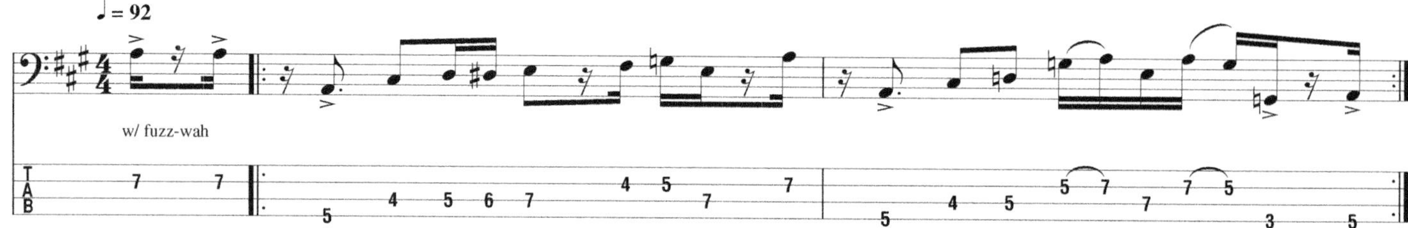

Solo Fills Excerpt

This section is a two-bar groove over B minor pentatonic played mostly in 2nd position. It's highly syncopated and densely mixed so, here again, you'll need to focus on the pickups (F♯–A–A♯) to the downbeat (B) of each two-bar phrase—and make sure you stick it on the 1! Play the hammer-on/pull-off phrases in measures 8, 12, and 16 in 4th position. Play the slide in measure 15 with your ring-pinky combo into 4th position so you'll be ready for the next measure.

TRACK 48

P
P

BASS NOTATION LEGEND

Bass music can be notated two different ways: on a *musical staff*, and in *tablature*.

THE MUSICAL STAFF shows pitches and rhythms and is divided by bar lines into measures. Pitches are named after the first seven letters of the alphabet.

TABLATURE graphically represents the bass fingerboard. Each horizontal line represents a string, and each number represents a fret.

Notes: G E C A / A F D B G

Strings: high G D A low E

3rd string, open — 2nd string, 2nd fret — 1st & 2nd strings open, played together

HAMMER-ON: Strike the first (lower) note with one finger, then sound the higher note (on the same string) with another finger by fretting it without picking.

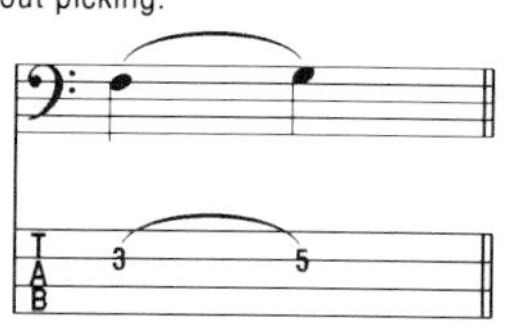

PULL-OFF: Place both fingers on the notes to be sounded. Strike the first note and without picking, pull the finger off to sound the second (lower) note.

LEGATO SLIDE: Strike the first note and then slide the same fret-hand finger up or down to the second note. The second note is not struck.

SHIFT SLIDE: Same as legato slide, except the second note is struck.

TRILL: Very rapidly alternate between the notes indicated by continuously hammering on and pulling off.

TREMOLO PICKING: The note is picked as rapidly and continuously as possible.

VIBRATO: The string is vibrated by rapidly bending and releasing the note with the fretting hand.

SHAKE: Using one finger, rapidly alternate between two notes on one string by sliding either a half-step above or below.

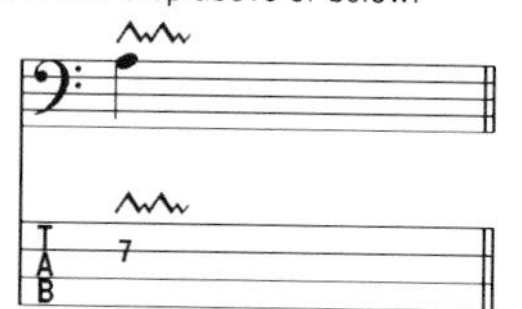

NATURAL HARMONIC: Strike the note while the fret hand lightly touches the string directly over the fret indicated.

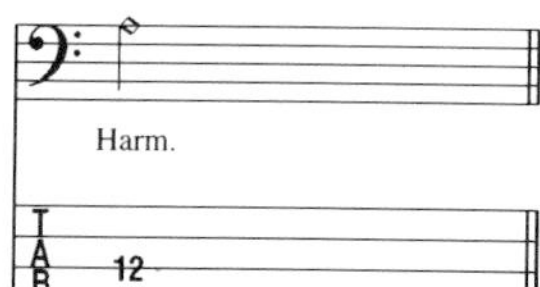

MUFFLED STRINGS: A percussive sound is produced by laying the fret hand across the string(s) without depressing them and striking them with the pick hand.

BEND: Strike the note and bend up the interval shown.

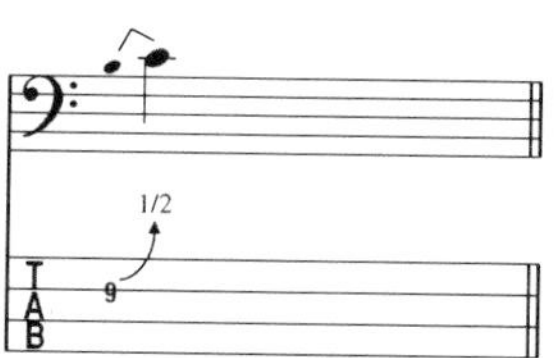

BEND AND RELEASE: Strike the note and bend up as indicated, then release back to the original note. Only the first note is struck.

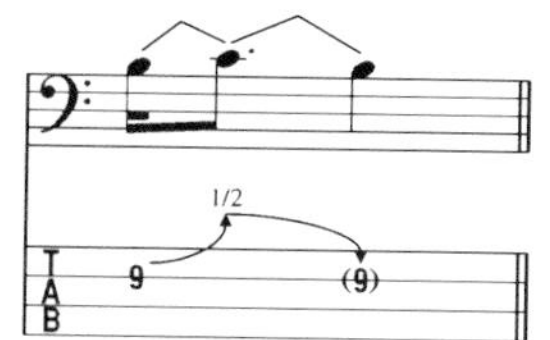

RIGHT-HAND TAP: Hammer ("tap") the fret indicated with the "pick-hand" index or middle finger and pull off to the note fretted by the fret hand.

LEFT-HAND TAP: Hammer ("tap") the fret indicated with the "fret-hand" index or middle finger.

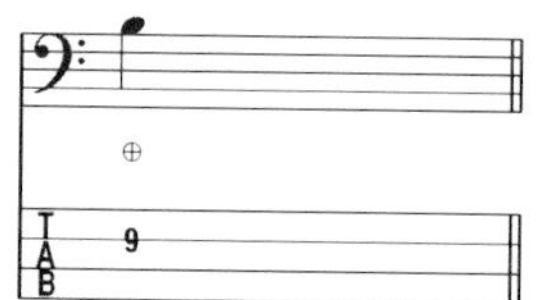

SLAP: Strike ("slap") string with right-hand thumb.

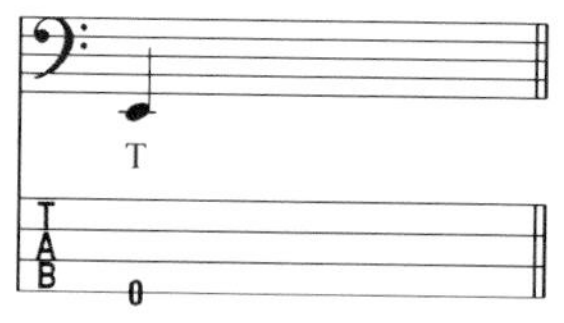

POP: Snap ("pop") string with right-hand index or middle finger.

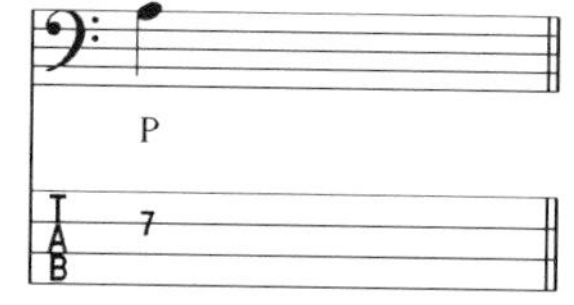

Additional Musical Definitions

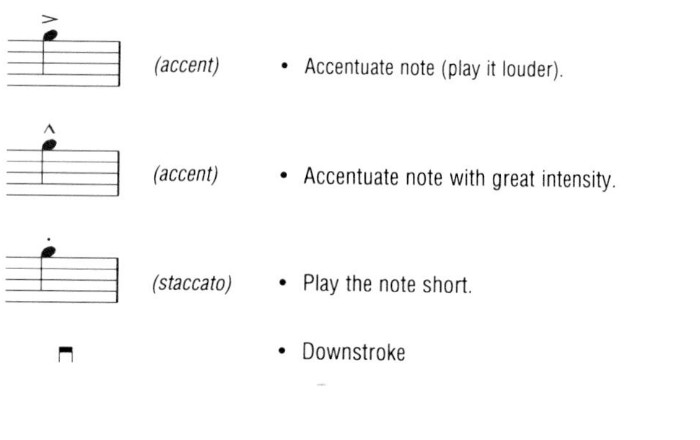

(accent) • Accentuate note (play it louder).

(accent) • Accentuate note with great intensity.

(staccato) • Play the note short.

• Downstroke

• Upstroke

D.S. al Coda • Go back to the sign (𝄋), then play until the measure marked "***To Coda***," then skip to the section labelled "**Coda**."

D.C. al Fine • Go back to the beginning of the song and play until the measure marked "***Fine***" (end).

Bass Fig. • Label used to recall a recurring pattern.

Fill • Label used to identify a brief melodic figure which is to be inserted into the arrangement.

tacet • Instrument is silent (drops out).

• Repeat measures between signs.

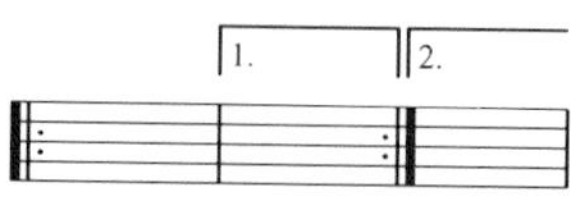

• When a repeated section has different endings, play the first ending only the first time and the second ending only the second time.

NOTE: Tablature numbers in parentheses mean:

1. The note is being sustained over a system (note in standard notation is tied), or
2. The note is sustained, but a new articulation (such as a hammer-on, pull-off, slide or vibrato) begins.